Created by Wild Pages Press 2017

Made in the USA
Monee, IL
10 December 2022

20614814R00085